7/98

SERVING YOUR COUNTRY

THE UNITED STATES ARMY

by Michael Green

Content Consultant:
Colonel Milton B. Halsey Jr.
United States Army (retired)

CAPSTONE
HIGH/LOW BOOKS
an imprint of Capstone Press

C A P S T O N E   P R E S S

818 North Willow Street • Mankato, Minnesota 56001
http://www.capstone-press.com

Library of Congress Cataloging-in-Publication Data
Green, Michael, 1952-
    The United States Army/by Michael Green.
    p. cm. -- (Serving your country)
    Includes bibliographical references (p. 44) and index.
    Summary: An introduction to the history, organization, function, equipment, and future of the United States Army.
    ISBN 1-56065-688-3
    1. United States. Army--Juvenile literature. [1. United States. Army.]
I. Title. II. Series

UA25.G79 1998
355.3'0973--dc21

                               97-40520
                                  CIP
                                    AC

Editorial credits:
Editor, Timothy Larson; cover design and illustrations, James Franklin; photo research, Michelle L. Norstad
Photo credits:
Archive Photos, 47; Earl Young, 18; Nikola Solil, 24; Yun Suk Bong, 38
The Boeing Company, 36
Michael Green, cover
National Archives, 10, 12
Unicorn Stock Photos/Aneal Vohra, 16
United Defense, 30
U.S. Army, 4, 8, 15, 20, 22, 26, 28, 32
U.S. Department of Defense, 34, 41

Table of Contents

Chapter 1
The U.S. Army

The United States Army is a branch of the U.S. military. A branch is one part of a large group. The U.S. Army is the oldest of the country's armed forces. The army has defended and served the United States for more than 200 years. Defend means to protect.

The U.S. Army's main job is to provide troops and equipment for land battles. The army provides the majority of the ground forces that fight during wartime. It also provides troops and equipment for air missions. A mission is a military task.

Peacetime

In peacetime, the army keeps its personnel organized, trained, and equipped for war. Personnel are the people who work for the army. The army provides ongoing training of military officers and enlisted personnel. Enlisted

The U.S. Army has defended and served the United States for more than 200 years.

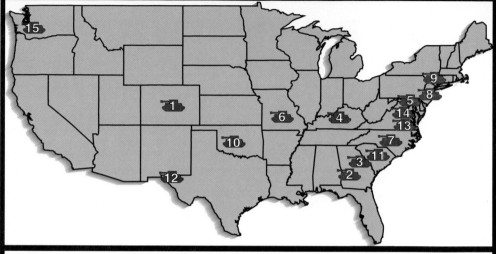

IMPORTANT U.S. ARMY POSTS

1) Ft. Carson, CO	5) Ft. Meade, MD	9) U.S. Military Academy, NY	13) Ft. Lee, VA
2) Ft. Benning, GA	6) Ft. Leonard Wood, MO	10) Ft. Sill, OK	14) Ft. Myer, VA
3) Ft. Gordon, GA	7) Ft. Bragg, NC	11) Ft. Jackson, SC	15) Ft. Lewis, WA
4) Ft. Knox, KY	8) Ft. Dix, NJ	12) Ft. Bliss, TX	

personnel are the people in the armed forces who are not officers. Training includes military and career skills.

The U.S. Army also provides non-military services during peacetime. It helps with humanitarian and peace-keeping missions around the world. Humanitarian means done for human good.

The army helps police fight the trade of illegal drugs. The army also conducts some police training.

Personnel

About 495,000 men and women serve in the U.S. Army. Men serve in positions ranging from infantry soldiers to officers. Infantry soldiers are soldiers trained to fight on foot. Women serve in many of the same positions as the men. But they cannot serve in all areas of active combat. Combat is fighting between militaries.

Most army soldiers are active-duty soldiers. Active-duty soldiers are full-time soldiers. They serve at army posts in the United States and around the world. They work, train, and stay ready for combat. Other soldiers are army reserves. Reserves are soldiers that stay ready for active duty. But they are not full-time soldiers.

Structure

The U.S. Army divides its troops into three arms. An arm is part of a branch of the military. The arms are the combat arm, the combat support arm, and the combat-service-support arm. Support means help.

The combat arm is the fighting part of the army. Its soldiers fight on the front lines. A front line is the area nearest enemy fire. Some of the

combat arm's soldiers operate deep within enemy territory.

The combat support arm manages and supports the combat arm during battle. It provides building crews and communication systems. Communication is the sharing of information. The combat support arm gathers information about enemies. It also provides help with supplies.

The combat-service-support arm provides support for the other two arms. It is responsible for directing supplies and transportation. Transportation is the system and means of moving people and supplies. The combat-service-support arm is also responsible for medical care and legal services. Legal means having to do with the law. This arm also handles the army's finances.

Soldiers in the army's combat arm fight on the front lines.

Chapter 2
History

The history of the United States Army starts with the Revolutionary War (1775-1783). The army fought the British army and helped the colonies win their freedom from Great Britain.

The U.S. Army fought in many wars after the Revolutionary War. It grew to become the United States' largest fighting force. Today, the army remains ready to defend the United States.

The Revolutionary War

On June 14, 1775, the Continental Congress passed a law that created the Continental army. This was the U.S. Army's earliest name. The Continental Congress was the group of leaders that made laws for the American colonies.

George Washington was the Continental army's first general and leader. Washington and his generals had less than 5,000 soldiers early in the Revolutionary War. Thousands of men joined the Continental army as the war continued.

George Washington was the Continental army's first general and leader.

In World War II, U.S. Army troops fought ground battles throughout Europe.

The Continental army fought in many famous battles including Lexington, Concord, and Bunker Hill. The army won its first victory at the Battle of Fort Ticonderoga in 1777. Later, the Continental army defeated the British Army during the Battle of Yorktown. The battle lasted from September to October in 1781. The Continental army's victory helped the colonies win the Revolutionary War.

The Civil War

The Civil War (1861-1865) was a difficult time for the U.S. Army. Many southern states left the United States during the Civil War. The states formed a separate country called the Confederate States of America. Some of the U.S. Army's officers and troops left to join the Confederate army.

Men who had been in the U.S. Army fought each other during the Civil War. Thousands of soldiers died on both sides during battles such as Bull Run, Shiloh, and Gettysburg. In April 1865, the Confederate army surrendered.

World Wars

In 1917, the United States entered World War I (1914-1918). The United States entered the war to help France and Britain fight Germany and its allies. Allies are countries that work together.

More than four million soldiers served in the U.S. Army during World War I. The army's infantry helped fight the ground war. Its pilots fought air battles over Europe. More than 53,000 U.S. soldiers and airmen died helping to win the war.

On December 7, 1941, the Japanese military attacked Pearl Harbor, Hawaii. The attack brought the United States into World War II (1939-1945).

The United States military joined the allied forces to fight against Germany, Italy, and Japan.

The U.S. Army helped fight air and ground battles throughout Europe and in the Pacific Ocean area. Army troops fought at places like the Philippines, Guadalcanal, and Luzon in the Pacific. They also fought at places like Normandy in France and the Rhineland in Germany. More than 291,000 U.S. Army soldiers and airmen died helping to win the war.

The Korean and Vietnam Wars

The U.S. Army helped fight the Korean War (1950-1953) and the Vietnam War (1954-1975).

In Korea, army troops fought at places including Osan, Pusan, Seoul, and Pork Chop Hill. Army troops fought in many places in South Vietnam. Some of these places were the areas around Saigon, Da Nang, and An Loc.

The Korean and Vietnam wars were confusing. More than 57,000 U.S. Army troops died fighting the wars. But no sides clearly won.

The Gulf War

In August 1990, war started in the Middle East when Iraq's army attacked Kuwait. The attack

The U.S. government sent army troops to help Kuwait fight the Gulf War.

began the Gulf War (1991). The United States government decided to help Kuwait. It sent U.S. troops to help Kuwait and its allies fight the war.

The U.S. Army helped win the Gulf War. It built command centers. It provided leaders. It helped train allied soldiers. The army moved allied troops and supplies. Its soldiers made up a large part of the ground forces.

Chapter 3
Training and Ranks

People between 17 and 29 years old who are in good health may join the U.S. Army. The army also requires that most applicants be high school graduates. An applicant is a person who applies for military service.

Most people who join the army apply at recruiting offices. Army recruiters make sure applicants meet age, health, and education requirements. Recruiters also help applicants decide which jobs they could do in the army. Applicants enter the army as enlisted personnel.

Officers enter the army in three ways. Some officers enter the army after graduating from military school. Some officers enter the army after finishing Reserve Officer Training Corps (ROTC) programs. An ROTC program teaches its members military leadership skills while they attend college. Other

Most people who join the army apply at recruiting offices.

Some officers train as cadets at the U.S. Military Academy in West Point, New York.

officers enter the army after finishing officer candidate school.

New enlisted personnel and officers agree to serve at least one tour of duty. A tour of duty is a set amount of service time. The average tour of duty for enlisted personnel is three to four years. The average tour of duty for officers is four to six years. Many soldiers serve more than one tour of duty. Serving longer lets soldiers increase their rank, responsibilities, and pay.

Officer Training

Some officers train as cadets at the U.S. Military Academy. A cadet is a military student. The academy is the army's military school. Cadets attend the academy for four years. They learn about the army. They learn army leadership skills. They also take regular classes like math and science. Cadets who graduate become officers.

Some officers train in the Army ROTC program. Students in the ROTC program attend college for four years. They learn regular subjects and military subjects. They also attend military classes at army posts for six weeks each summer.

Some enlisted personnel and college graduates attend officer candidate school. The army's officer candidate school is a series of tough training courses. The courses provide the basic skills needed for leadership. People who pass the courses become officers.

Officers receive more training when they earn higher ranks. New officers take the officer's basic course. They take the advanced officer's course after several years of service. Higher-ranking officers attend the Command and General Staff College and the Army War College. Sometimes the

Drill sergeants make recruits work hard during basic training.

army also sends officers to public colleges to learn special skills.

Enlisted Training

New enlisted personnel are called recruits. Recruits learn to be soldiers during basic training. The U.S. Army's basic training lasts eight weeks. Men and women train together.

Drill sergeants make recruits work hard during basic training. Recruits wake up early and train until late in the day. They do exercises. They go on long runs and marches. Recruits learn about weapons and practice using them. Recruits also learn about military rules and laws.

Most recruits receive specialist training after basic training. But they can request specialist training at anytime during their careers. Recruits learn how to perform certain army jobs during specialist training.

Ranks

The army has ten enlisted ranks. They range from recruit to sergeant major of the army. Enlisted personnel begin their careers as recruits. They earn higher ranks as they serve and receive more training. Enlisted personnel can also work their way up to the officer ranks.

There are eleven main officer ranks in the army. The ranks range from second lieutenant to general of the army. New officers start as second lieutenants. Officers may earn higher ranks by serving longer and receiving more training. Some officers with special training enter at higher ranks. Experienced doctors or lawyers may enter at the rank of captain.

The army gives enlisted personnel and officers pay raises when they earn new ranks. The army also gives them small pay raises every other year.

Chapter 4
Army Jobs

The U.S. Army has hundreds of jobs for enlisted personnel and officers. Officers and enlisted personnel often work together.

Each job is related to one of the army's different arms. Each job is also important to the army in peacetime and wartime.

Combat Jobs

The army's combat arm has six branches. The branches include the infantry branch, the field artillery branch, and the air-defense-artillery branch. They also include the armor branch, the aviation branch, and the Special Forces branch. All the branches of the combat arm train and fight together.

The infantry branch is made up of infantry soldiers. Infantry soldiers are the army's main fighting force. These soldiers fight directly with enemies during ground combat.

Infantry soldiers are the army's main fighting force.

Soldiers in the Military Police Corps patrol posts and enforce military law.

The field artillery branch supports the infantry. Field artillery soldiers fire cannons and missiles at enemy targets on land. A missile is an explosive that can fly long distances.

The air-defense-artillery branch protects the field artillery and infantry from enemy planes and missiles. Soldiers in this branch fire guns and shoot missiles at enemy planes.

The armor branch provides ground support for the infantry. Soldiers in the armor branch operate tanks. They attack enemy tanks and other targets on land.

The aviation branch is the army's air force. It provides air support for the ground forces. Many of the soldiers in this branch are pilots. Most army pilots fly helicopters.

The Special Forces branch is responsible for secret missions. Members of this branch are the army's best soldiers. They often work behind enemy lines. They spy on the enemy and destroy enemy structures. They also plan and make surprise attacks.

Combat Support Jobs

The combat support arm has four branches. The branches include the Corps of Engineers and the Military Police Corps. They also include Military Intelligence and the Signal Corps.

Soldiers in the Corps of Engineers plan and build structures. The Military Police Corps is the army's police force. Soldiers in the Military Police Corps patrol posts and enforce military law. Soldiers in Military Intelligence gather information about enemies.

Soldiers in the Quartermaster Corps control the army's supplies.

The Signal Corps is responsible for army communication. Soldiers in the Signal Corps set up and repair communication systems like telephones and radios.

Combat-Service-Support Jobs

The combat-service-support arm has six branches. The branches include the Transportation Corps, the Ordnance Corps, and the Quartermaster Corps. They also include the Finance Corps, the Medical Corps, and the Judge Advocate General's Corps. Soldiers in these branches usually do not work in combat zones.

Soldiers in the Transportation Corps control the army's transportation. They operate and repair many of the army's vehicles. A vehicle is a machine that carries people or supplies. Soldiers in the Ordnance Corps repair weapons. Soldiers in the Quartermaster Corps control the army's supplies.

Soldiers in the Finance Corps are responsible for the army's money. They keep financial records and pay soldiers. The Medical Corps provides medical care. Soldiers in the Medical Corps are doctors, nurses, and medics. A medic is a person who is trained to give medical help. Soldiers in the Judge Advocate General's Corps provide legal services. They serve as lawyers and other legal staff.

Chapter 5

Weapons and Equipment

The U.S. Army uses different weapons and equipment to carry out its combat missions. Soldiers and pilots use weapons and equipment to attack enemies and defend themselves.

Infantry Weapons

M-16 rifles are infantry soldiers' most important weapons. The M-16 is light. It only weighs about eight pounds (3.6 kilograms). This makes it easy to carry and handle. The M-16 is also powerful. It can fire one round at a time or three-round bursts. A round is a bullet. The M-16 has a range of 600 yards (549 meters).

The Squad Automatic Weapon (SAW) is the infantry's newest machine gun. The SAW is a hand-held machine gun. But it also has a bipod. A bipod is a two-legged stand. The bipod helps keep the SAW steady when fired. The SAW can

M-16 rifles are infantry soldiers' most important weapons.

The Paladin (right) is the field artillery's newest kind
of howitzer.

fire up to 750 rounds per minute. It has a range of
1,094 yards (1,000 meters).

Infantry soldiers attack enemy troops and
vehicles with mortars. A mortar is a short cannon
that shoots small, explosive shells. One of the
infantry's largest mortars can fire four shells per
minute up to 7,956 yards (7,275 meters).

Infantry soldiers use missiles to defend
themselves against enemy tanks and aircraft.
Stingers are one kind of missile infantry soldiers

use. Soldiers fire stingers from shoulder launchers. A launcher is a device that shoots some kinds of explosives. Stingers have ranges of one to five miles (1.6 to 8.1 kilometers).

Field Artillery Weapons

The field artillery and air-defense-artillery branches use long-range weapons to support the infantry during battle. These weapons allow field artillery soldiers to attack distant enemy targets.

Howitzers and missiles are the main kinds of long-range weapons. A howitzer is a cannon that shoots explosive shells long distances.

The Paladin is the field artillery's newest kind of howitzer. The Paladin is an armored vehicle with a built-in howitzer. Armor is a protective metal or plastic covering. The Paladin can shoot shells more than 19 miles (31 kilometers).

The Tactical Missile System is an important field artillery weapon. The field artillery uses the system against targets on land. Armored trucks carry the Tactical Missile System. This allows soldiers to move the systems quickly during battle. The Tactical Missile System has a range of more than 300 miles (480 kilometers).

The air-defense-artillery fires Patriot missiles at high-flying enemy aircraft and missiles. Patriot missiles have ranges up to 43 miles (69 kilometers).

Armor Branch Tanks

M1 and M1A1 Abrams tanks are the armor branch's main battle tanks. Each Abrams tank has machine guns and a large main gun. The main gun can fire shells up to three miles (4.8 kilometers). Abrams tanks weigh nearly 68 tons (61.2 metric tons). But they can travel up to 42 miles (67.6 kilometers) per hour.

The armor branch is also using a new kind of Abrams tank. The new tank is the M1A2 Abrams. It has a number of new features including thicker armor. The armor gives tank crews better protection during battle.

Aviation Branch Aircraft

Helicopters are the aviation branch's most important aircraft. The branch uses some helicopters for combat. It uses other helicopters as transport aircraft. Transport aircraft carry weapons, equipment, and troops.

M1 Abrams tanks are among the armor branch's main battle tanks.

The aviation branch uses several kinds of combat helicopters. Kiowa Warriors and Apache gunships are two important kinds. The aviation branch uses Kiowa Warriors to scout for enemy aircraft, troops, and structures. It also uses Kiowa Warriors as attack aircraft. Kiowa Warriors have guns, rockets, and missiles.

Apache gunships are the aviation branch's main attack helicopters. Each Apache gunship has a powerful machine gun and Hellfire missiles. Hellfire missiles can destroy enemy aircraft, tanks, structures, and ships.

Blackhawk and Chinook helicopters are the aviation branch's main transport helicopters. The Blackhawk can carry 11 soldiers. It can also lift and carry equipment and vehicles.

The Chinook is the aviation branch's largest transport helicopter. It can carry 44 soldiers. It can also lift and carry large vehicles and weapons.

The U.S. Army uses Kiowa Warriors to scout for and attack enemies.

BLADES

ENGINES

COCKPIT

GUN

MISSILES

APACHE GUNSHIP

TAIL

TAIL SECTION

Chapter 6
The Future

Today, some U.S. leaders believe there is little chance of major wars. They also believe there is no need for a large U.S. military. Because of this, the U.S. government has cut some funding to the country's military.

The U.S. Army has become smaller because of these cuts. It has closed some of its posts and reduced the number of its troops. But the army is still strong. It continues to defend the United States and help its allies. Its plans for the future include new goals and new equipment.

New Goals

The army has two main goals for the future. It wants to develop the best information systems. It also wants to increase the speed of its combat operations. Reaching these goals will help the army end wars quickly and reduce the loss of life.

Better information systems will help the army gather important facts about enemies. Facts may

The U.S. Army will continue to help defend the United States and its allies.

include enemy locations, supply routes, and command centers. Increased speed will help the army defeat enemies quickly.

New Equipment

The U.S. Army is working on new equipment to help it reach its goals. The equipment includes spacecraft, aircraft, and ground combat devices.

The Global Positioning System (GPS) is one of the army's important projects. The GPS is a group of satellites. A satellite is a spacecraft that orbits Earth.

The army wants to use GPS satellites to gather information. The GPS satellites can take pictures of Earth's surface. They can also pick up many radio and telephone communications. These satellites could help the army spy on enemies. They could also help the army send and receive information more quickly.

The army is also planning aircraft and vehicles that do not need crews. Information from GPS satellites, computers, and radar will help guide the aircraft and vehicles. Radar is machinery that sends out radio waves to locate and guide objects.

Personal ground combat computers may replace maps.

The army is also working on new equipment for soldiers. Personal ground combat computers are an important army project. The computers may replace maps. These computers are small and light so soldiers can carry them. They receive information from GPS satellites. They can show soldiers their locations on battlefields. They can also show the locations of enemies.

WORDS TO KNOW

allies (AL-eyes)—countries that work together
applicant (AP-luh-kuhnt)—a person who applies for military service
branch (BRANCH)—one part of a large group
cadet (kuh-DET)—a military student
combat (KOM-bat)—fighting between militaries
communication (kuh-myoo-nuh-KAY-shun)— the sharing of information
Continental Congress (KON-tuh-nen-tuhl KON-gress)—the group of leaders that made laws for the American colonies
front line (FRUHNT LINE)—the area nearest enemy fire
howitzer (HOU-uht-sur)—a cannon that shoots explosive shells long distances
humanitarian (hyoo-man-uh-TER-ee-uhn)— done for human good
medic (MED-ik)—a person who is trained to give medical help
missile (MISS-uhl)—an explosive that can fly long distances

mission (MISH-uhn)—a military task

mortar (MOR-tur)—a short cannon that shoots small, explosive shells

personnel (purss-uh-NEL)—the people who work for the army

radar (RAY-dar)—machinery that sends out radio waves to locate and guide objects

recruiting office (ri-KROOT-ing OF-iss)—a place where people apply to join the military

reserves (ri-ZURVZ)—troops that stay ready for active duty but are not full-time soldiers

Reserve Officer Training Corps (ri-ZURV OF-uh-sur TRANE-ing KOR)—a program that teaches its members military leadership skills while they attend college; ROTC

satellite (SAT-uh-lite)—a spacecraft that orbits Earth

tour of duty (TOOR UHV DOO-tee)—a set amount of service time

transportation (transs-pur-TAY-shuhn)—the system and means of moving people and supplies

TO LEARN MORE

Green, Michael. *Military Trucks*. Mankato, Minn.: Capstone Press, 1997.

Hole, Dorothy. *The Army and You.* New York: Crestwood House, 1993.

Meltzer, Milton. *Weapons and Warfare: From the Stone Age to the Space Age.* New York: HarperCollins, 1996.

Ray, Delia. *Behind the Blue and Gray: The Soldier's Life in the Civil War.* New York: Puffin, 1996.

USEFUL ADDRESSES

U.S. Army Aviation Museum
P.O. Box 610
Fort Rucker, AL 36362

National Infantry Museum
Attn: ATZB-PTN
Fort Benning, GA 31905-5272

U.S. Army Field Artillery Museum
Building 437
Quanah Road
Fort Sill, OK 73503-5123

U.S. Army Public Affairs
1500 Army Pentagon
Washington, DC 20310-1500

INTERNET SITES

ArmyLINK: U.S. Army Public Affairs
http://www.dtic.mil/armylink/

Military History
http://www.cfcsc.dnd.ca/links/milhist/index.html

Welcome to the Center of Military History
http://www.army.mil/cmh-pg/

Welcome to the U.S. Army Homepage
http://www.army.mil/

The U.S. Army helps with humanitarian and peace-keeping missions around the world.

INDEX